+MATH FOR MARTIANS+

Planet Omicron

Illustrated by Jane Tassie ☄ Written by Julie Ferris

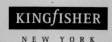

KING*fisher*

NEW YORK

KINGFISHER
Larousse Kingfisher Chambers Inc.
95 Madison Avenue
New York, New York 10016

First published in 2000
10 9 8 7 6 5 4 3 2 1

1TR/0100/TWP/FR/170ARM

LIBRARY OF CONGRESS CATALOGING-IN-PUBLICATION DATA
Ferris, Julie.
   Planet Omicron / by Julie Ferris; illustrated
by Jane Tassie.—1st ed.
      p. cm.— (Math for martians)
   Summary: Help Zeno the Martian solve the
mathematical puzzles that he encounters on
his visit to Planet Omicron.
   ISBN 0-7534-5277-4 (pb)
   1. Mathematical recreations—
Juvenile literature. [1. Puzzles.
2. Mathematical recreations.]
I. Tassie, Jane ill. II. Title.
III. Series.

QA95 F47 2000
793.7'4—dc21
                  99-048394

Coordinating editor: Laura Marshall

Printed in Singapore

Contents

Zeno lives with his mother in Zala, a small city on Mars. Zeno likes adventure, but he is not always very brave. Zeno's pet is named Zarf. He is a bernum from planet Zib.

Zormella is Zeno's cyberpal. She lives in Myria City on planet Numis. She is very practical and always carries a backpack full of useful things.

Sallulah Snaffle is a space pirate captain on planet Omicron. She will do anything to find the treasure!

3

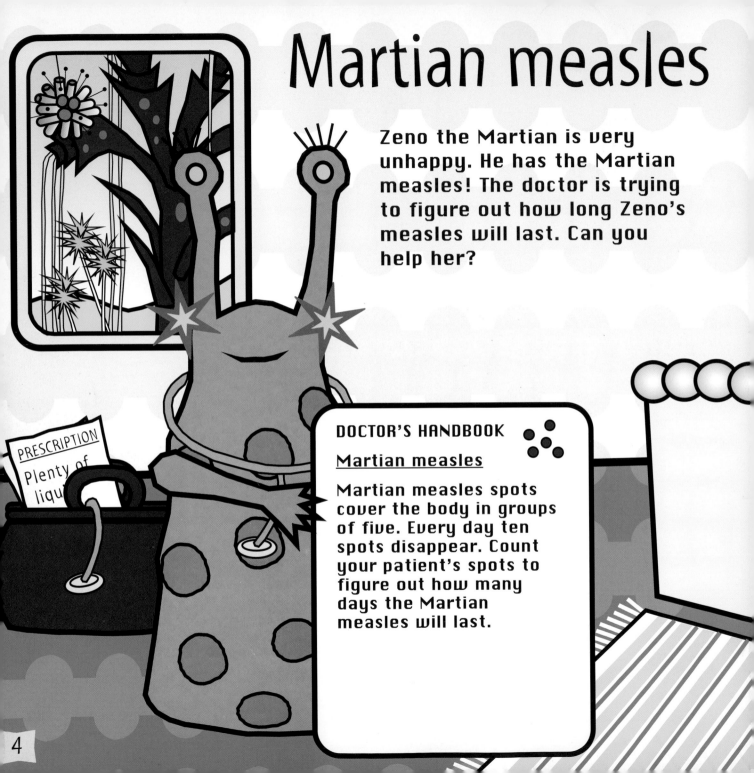

Martian measles

Zeno the Martian is very unhappy. He has the Martian measles! The doctor is trying to figure out how long Zeno's measles will last. Can you help her?

PRESCRIPTION
Plenty of
liqu

DOCTOR'S HANDBOOK

Martian measles

Martian measles spots cover the body in groups of five. Every day ten spots disappear. Count your patient's spots to figure out how many days the Martian measles will last.

"Don't worry," says Zeno's mother. "Zarf will play with you, and I have a surprise for you when you get better!"

BARP JUICE

Surprise!

At last, the spots are gone. Zeno is excited about his surprise. "Be patient," his mother tells him. "You will find out soon."

Zeno goes outside to play zarzar arrows. He throws his arrows at the target. To score points, the arrow tips have to stick to the target's score areas.

If he scores 100 points, a drawer in the target opens. Inside is yummy zarzar candy.

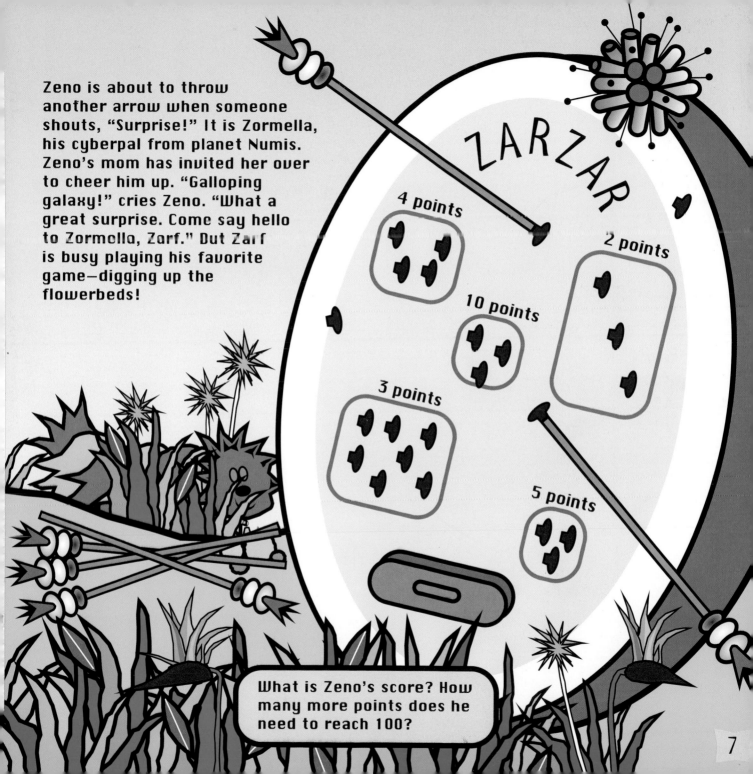

Zeno is about to throw another arrow when someone shouts, "Surprise!" It is Zormella, his cyberpal from planet Numis. Zeno's mom has invited her over to cheer him up. "Galloping galaxy!" cries Zeno. "What a great surprise. Come say hello to Zormella, Zarf." But Zarf is busy playing his favorite game—digging up the flowerbeds!

ZARZAR

4 points

2 points

10 points

3 points

5 points

What is Zeno's score? How many more points does he need to reach 100?

Treasure map

Zarf has found something in the flowerbed. It is a long, tube-shaped container. Inside is a map with strange numbers taped on it.

	A	B	C	D
1	O		T	Kora
2	A	Brint	Tully	E
3	H		S	Kal / S
4	R	X (Kelpa)	T / P	M
5	K		C	D

"It is a secret code," says Zormella. "If we write down the letter in square 4B, then the letter in square 5D, and so on, we can crack it." Can you?

"It must be a treasure map," says Zeno. "Let's find the treasure!"

It takes four Martian hours to fly from Mars to planet Omicron. There are 12 Martian minutes in every Martian hour. How many Martian minutes will the trip take?

PLANET OMICRON MAP COMPANY

○ OMEGA ISLANDS ○

1
2
3
4
5

SECRET CODE
4B / 5D
2B 4A 5A 4D
/ 1C 3A 3D /
3B 5C 1A 4C

Property of Captain Silex Snaffle

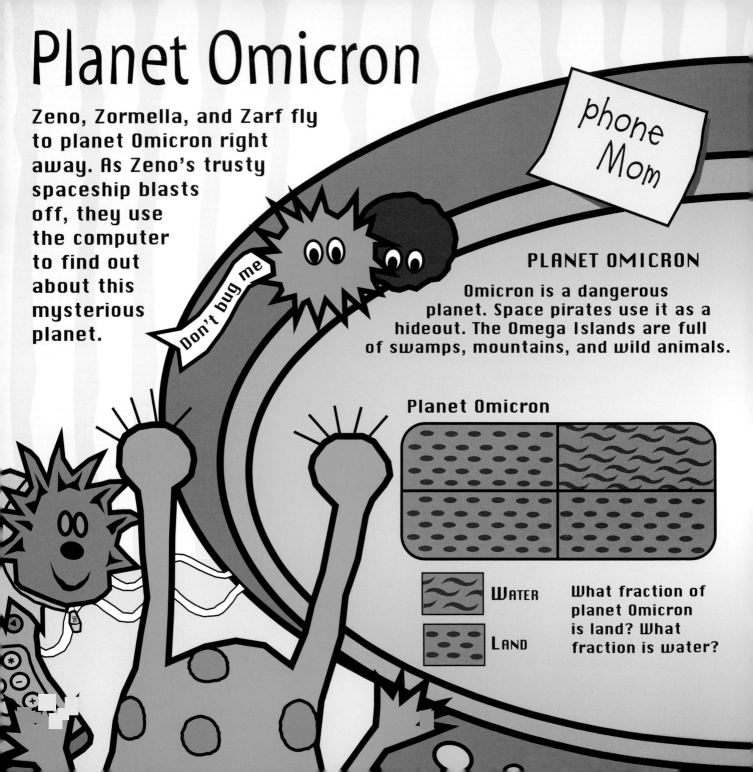

Planet Omicron

Zeno, Zormella, and Zarf fly to planet Omicron right away. As Zeno's trusty spaceship blasts off, they use the computer to find out about this mysterious planet.

phone Mom

Don't bug me

PLANET OMICRON

Omicron is a dangerous planet. Space pirates use it as a hideout. The Omega Islands are full of swamps, mountains, and wild animals.

Planet Omicron

WATER

LAND

What fraction of planet Omicron is land? What fraction is water?

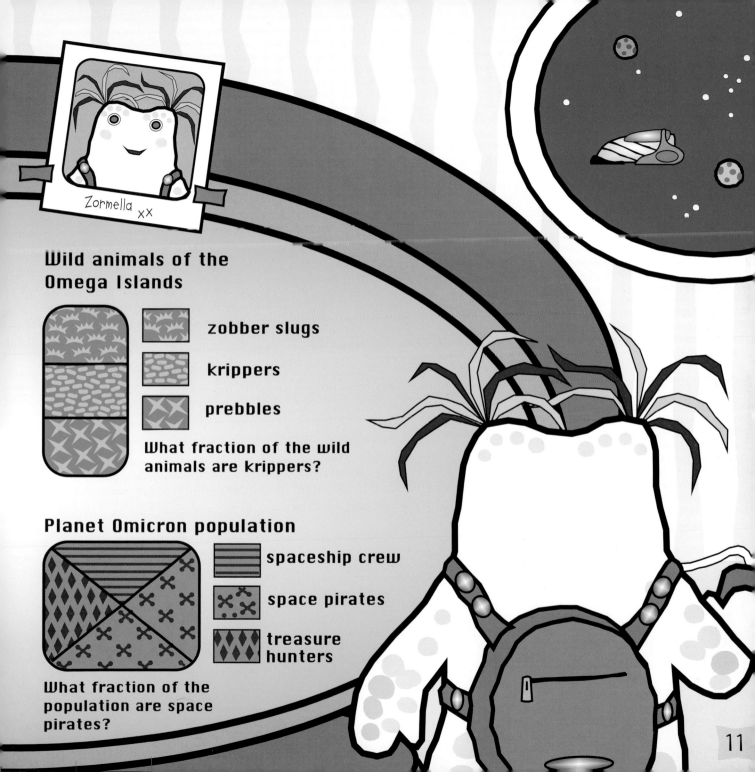

Wild animals of the Omega Islands

zobber slugs

krippers

prebbles

What fraction of the wild animals are krippers?

Planet Omicron population

spaceship crew

space pirates

treasure hunters

What fraction of the population are space pirates?

Zormella xx

11

Supplies

The spaceship lands on Kora Island. There is a small store there. Zeno and Zormella can buy what they need to find the buried treasure.

"We need rope, two shovels, and some food," says Zormella. "We only have 300 omes," says Zeno. "I hope it is enough."

Do Zeno and Zormella have enough money to pay for their supplies?

SPACE
PRUNES
ON SALE

How much money do they need to buy everything
shown here? Will they get any change?

2 SHOVELS
50 omes
each

1 ROPE
20 omes

6 CARTONS OF
BARP JUICE
5 omes
each

9 FRAPPLE
MUFFINS
5 omes
each

12 ZARZAR
CANDIES
2 omes
each

BARP
JUICE

Space ferry

The treasure is buried on Kelpa Island. Zeno, Zormella, and Zarf will take a space ferry there. How much will their ticket cost?

TICKETS

Brint

Aliens	20 omes
Pets	10 omes

Tully

Aliens	10 omes
Pets	5 omes

Kelpa

Aliens	25 omes
Pets	15 omes

Kal

Aliens	30 omes
Pets	20 omes

The shapes on their ticket tell them which space ferry to board. Can you find the space ferry with the matching shapes on it?

SPACE FERRY TICKET

Admit:
2 aliens
1 pet

On the trail

Kelpa Island is a dangerous place!
It is covered with swamps where
zobber slugs, krippers, and prebbles
live. Zeno, Zormella, and Zarf are very
nervous. They hear many strange
noises along the way.

13

20

23

15

18

6

START
21

12

4

43

17

35

FINISH
24

30

9

3

27

10

Soon they have to cross a slimy swamp. It is full of fierce krippers and prebbles. Many of the stepping stones are covered in slippery zobber slug slime. The only way across is by stepping on the rocks that are in the three times table. Can you help them cross the swamp?

17

Capture

Whew! Zeno, Zormella, and Zarf cross the swamp safely. On the other side is a path, with snakelike kelpa vines on both sides. Zeno checks the map. "I think we are almost there," he says.

"What is that noise?" asks Zormella. "It is coming from the kelpa vines."

Suddenly, they are surrounded by space pirates! One of the pirates steps forward. "I am Captain Sallulah Snaffle," she cries. "You are now my prisoners!"

The space pirates grab Zeno, Zormella, and Zarf and take them to their pirate spaceship.

How many pirates are there? How many are carrying swords with straight edges? How many are carrying swords with wavy edges? Are there more pirates with red hats or yellow hats?

Pirate spaceship

Captain Sallulah Snaffle snatches the treasure map from Zeno. "My map!" Zeno cries.

"Your map?" says Sallulah. "My grandfather, Captain Silex Snaffle, drew this map. He was a tough and terrible pirate. He also made the sweetest waffles in the whole universe. Everyone wanted his recipe, but he wanted to keep it a secret. He buried the recipe on Kelpa Island. But he lost the map!"

Sallulah held the map tighter. "For years I have looked for the recipe. I have trapped treasure hunters and taken their maps. At last I have found the right one!"

"Lock them in the laboratory," says Sallulah to one of the space pirates. "Then we will go find the recipe." The pirate pushes Zeno, Zormella, and Zarf into the laboratory.

To lock the door, the pirate has to type in a code. Can you figure out the code?

LABORATORY DOOR CODE

The first number is 4 less than 2×8

The second number is 3 more than 4×5

The third number is 6 less than 9×3

The fourth number is 10 more than 7+8

The fifth number is less than 2×5 but more than 4+4

The laboratory

Zeno, Zormella, and Zarf are trapped in the laboratory. They bang on the door, but no one lets them out. "What do we do now?" Zormella wonders.

"Well, I am hungry," says Zeno. "I think we should eat our frapple muffins." Zormella takes the food out of her backpack. There are 9 frapple muffins, 6 cartons of barp juice, and 12 zarzar candies.

If Zeno, Zormella, and Zarf all get the same number of muffins, how many will each get? How many juice cartons? How many candies?

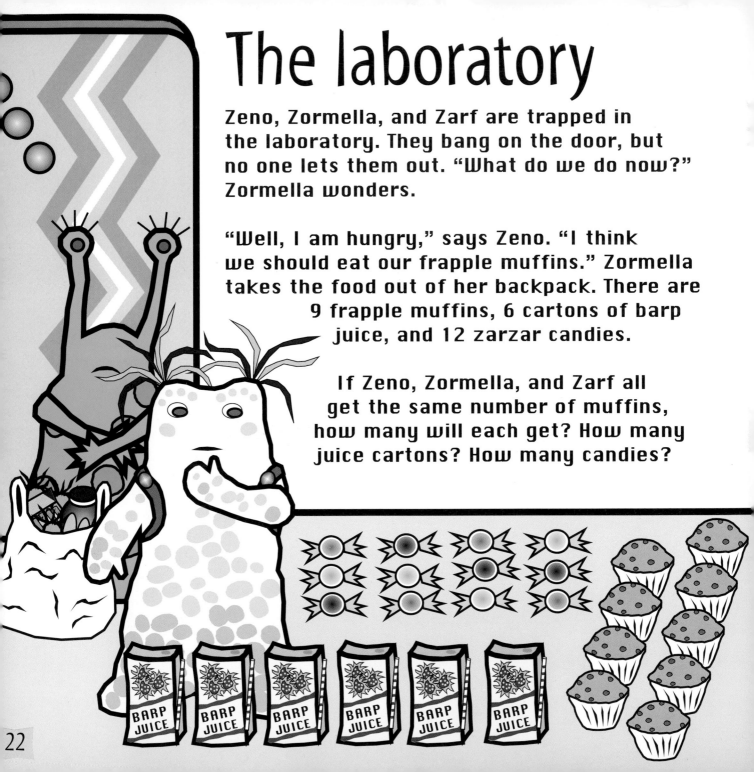

After their snack, Zeno and Zormella look for a way to escape. Zeno finds a formula book. Inside is a formula for blowing up locks. "If we make this formula, we can blow up the lock on the door and escape," he says. How many of each ingredient will they need?

EXPLODING LOCKS ~ FORMULA ~

You will need:
- bibble sticks
- orfeel leaves
- poddles
- monchas

To find out how many of each ingredient you need: Look at the chart below. Each letter has a number. Add the numbers that go with each of the letters in an ingredient's name. For example, barps: 2+1+8+6+9=26. You would need 26 barps.

A	B	C	D	E	F	G	H	I	J	K	L
1	2	3	4	5	6	7	8	9	10	1	2

M	N	O	P	Q	R	S	T	U	V
3	4	5	6	7	8	9	10	1	2

W	X	Y	Z
3	4	5	6

Mix all the ingredients. Rub on the lock and stand back!

Back on the trail

KABOOM! The lock explodes. Zeno, Zormella, and Zarf run from the pirate spaceship.

Farther down the path, the pirates are trying to read the treasure map. "I know how we can stop them," Zormella whispers. She takes the rope out of her backpack. She gives one end to Zarf. Zarf runs around and around the pirates. Then he and Zormella pull on the rope until the space pirates are all tied up.

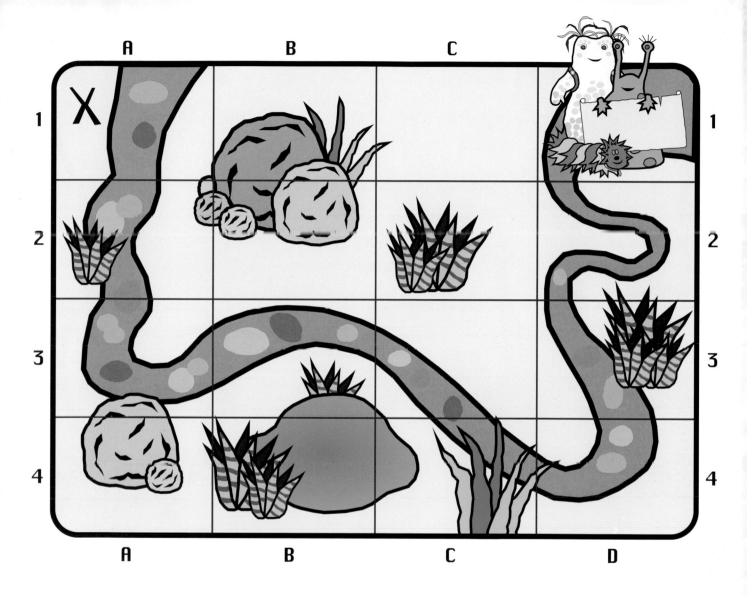

Zeno grabs the map from Sallulah. How do they get to the treasure? It is buried under the spot marked X. They are in grid square 1D. What other squares will they go through on their way to the treasure?

Treasure!

X marks the spot! Zeno and Zormella dig and dig. Finally they hit something hard. It is a metal box. There is a message inside: "Follow the number maze to discover the ingredients. Mix together and fry for ten minutes."

MESSAGE

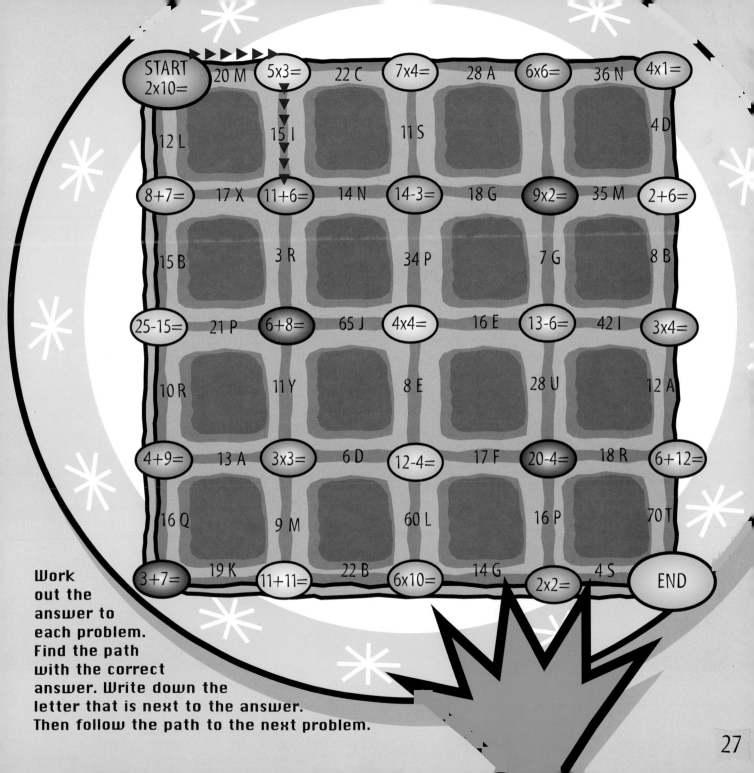

START
2x10=

20 M | 5x3= | 22 C | 7x4= | 28 A | 6x6= | 36 N | 4x1=

12 L | 15 I | 11 S | 4 D

8+7= | 17 X | 11+6= | 14 N | 14-3= | 18 G | 9x2= | 35 M | 2+6=

15 B | 3 R | 34 P | 7 G | 8 B

25-15= | 21 P | 6+8= | 65 J | 4x4= | 16 E | 13-6= | 42 I | 3x4=

10 R | 11 Y | 8 E | 28 U | 12 A

4+9= | 13 A | 3x3= | 6 D | 12-4= | 17 F | 20-4= | 18 R | 6+12=

16 Q | 9 M | 60 L | 16 P | 70 T

3+7= | 19 K | 11+11= | 22 B | 6x10= | 14 G | 2x2= | 4 S | END

Work out the answer to each problem. Find the path with the correct answer. Write down the letter that is next to the answer. Then follow the path to the next problem.

27

New friends

"I can't wait to try Captain Snaffle's space waffles!" says Zormella. "But what about the space pirates?" asks Zeno. "We can't leave them!" The space pirates promise to behave. Zeno and Zormella untie them. And to show there are no hard feelings, Zeno invites his new friends to eat waffles on his spaceship.

Answers

4–5 Martian measles

ZENO'S MEASLES WILL LAST FOR **5** DAYS.

There are 10 groups with 5 spots each. This makes 50 spots in all (10×5=50 or (5+5+5+5+5+5+5+5+5+5=50). Every day 10 spots disappear. There are 5 tens in 50 (10+10+10+10+10=50), so the measles will last for 5 days.

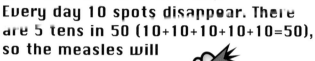

6–7 Surprise!

ZENO HAS SCORED **88** POINTS.
4 arrow tips in the 4-point area scores 16 points (4×4=16 or 4+4+4+4=16). 3 arrow tips in the 10-point area scores 30 points (3×10=30 or 10+10+10=30). 3 arrow tips in the 2-point area scores 6 points (3×2=6 or 2+2+2=6). 7 arrow tips in the 3-point area scores 21 points (7×3=21 or 3+3+3+3+3+3+3=21). 3 arrow tips in the 5-point area scores 15 points (3×5=15 or 5+5+5=15). Add up all the points to find the total: 16+30+6+21+15=88.
ZENO NEEDS **12** MORE POINTS TO REACH **100**.
100-88=12.

8–9 Treasure map

THE CODE READS: " X MARKS THE SPOT."
THE JOURNEY WILL TAKE **48** MARTIAN MINUTES.
There are 12 Martian minutes in every Martian hour. The journey takes 4 Martian hours (4×12=48 or (12+12+12+12=48).

10–11 Planet Omicron

¾ OF PLANET **O**MICRON IS LAND. ¼ IS WATER.
The box is divided into 4 parts. 3 parts have the symbol for land in them. 1 part has the symbol for water in it.
⅓ OF THE WILD ANIMALS ARE KRIPPERS.
The box is divided into 3 parts. 1 part has the symbol for krippers.
½ OF THE POPULATION ARE SPACE PIRATES.
The box is divided into 4 parts. 2 parts contain the symbol for space pirates. 2 is one half of 4 (2×2=4 or 2+2=4).

Don't bug me

12–13 Supplies

YES, ZENO AND ZORMELLA HAVE ENOUGH MONEY. THEY NEED **219** OMES TO BUY EVERYTHING.

2 shovels at 50 omes each cost 100 omes ($2 \times 50 = 100$ or $50 + 50 = 100$); 1 rope at 20 omes each costs 20 omes ($1 \times 20 = 20$); **6 cartons of barp juice at 5 omes each cost 30 omes ($6 \times 5 = 30$ or $5 + 5 + 5 + 5 + 5 + 5 = 30$); 9 frapple muffins at 5 omes each cost 45 omes ($9 \times 5 = 45$ or $5 + 5 + 5 + 5 + 5 + 5 + 5 + 5 + 5 = 45$); 12 zarzar candies at 2 omes each cost 24 omes ($12 \times 2 = 24$ or $2 + 2 + 2 + 2 + 2 + 2 + 2 + 2 + 2 + 2 + 2 + 2 = 24$). All their shopping costs 219 omes ($100 + 20 + 30 + 45 + 24 = 219$). They have 300 omes.** THEY WILL GET **81** OMES IN CHANGE. **$300 - 219 = 81$ omes**

14–15 Space ferry

THEIR TICKET COSTS **65** OMES. **Zeno and Zormella will pay 25 omes each. Zarf's fare is 15 omes. The total fare is 65 omes** ($25 + 25 + 15 = 65$).

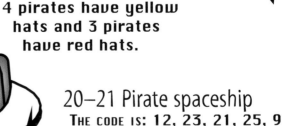

16–17 On the trail

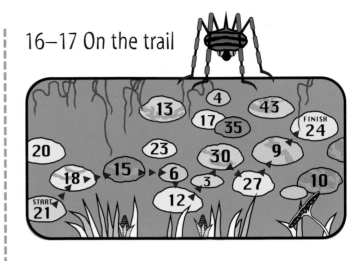

18–19 Capture

THERE ARE **8** SPACE PIRATES (INCLUDING SALLULAH SNAFFLE). **2** SPACE PIRATES ARE CARRYING SWORDS WITH STRAIGHT EDGES. **4** SPACE PIRATES ARE CARRYING SWORDS WITH WAVY EDGES. THERE ARE MORE PIRATES WITH YELLOW HATS THAN WITH RED HATS. **4 pirates have yellow hats and 3 pirates have red hats.**

20–21 Pirate spaceship

THE CODE IS: **12, 23, 21, 25, 9. The first number is 4 less than 2×8: $2 \times 8 = 16$ (or $8 + 8 = 16$). $16 - 4 = 12$**

The second number is
3 more than 4×5:
4×5=20 (or 5+5+5+5=20).
20+3=23
The third number is 6
less than 9×3: 9×3=27
(or 3+3+3+3+3+3+3+3+3=27).
27-6=21
The fourth number is 10 more
than 7+8:
7+8=15.
15+10=25
The fifth number is less than 2×5
but more than 4+4:
2×5=10 (or 5+5=10).
4+4=8
9 is the only number that is less than
10 and more than 8.

22–23 The Laboratory

THEY CAN EACH HAVE 3 FRAPPLE MUFFINS.
There are 9 muffins to be shared by
3 aliens. They can each have 3 frapple
muffins (9÷3=3 or 3+3+3=9).
THEY CAN EACH HAVE 2 CARTONS OF JUICE.
There are 6 cartons of barp juice to
be shared by 3 aliens. They can each
have 2 cartons (6÷3=2 or 3+3=6).
THEY CAN EACH HAVE 4 ZARZAR CANDIES.
There are 12 zarzar candies to be
shared by the 3 aliens. They can
each have 4 candies (12÷3=4 or
3+3+3+3=12).

THEY WILL NEED 63 BIBBLE STICKS.
B=2 I=9 B=2 B=2 L=2 E=5
S=9 T=10 I=9 C=3 K=1 S=9
2+9+2+2+2+5+9+10+9+3+1+9=63
THEY WILL NEED 55 ORFEEL LEAVES.
O=5 R=8 F=6 E=5 E=5 L=2 L=2
E=5 A=1 V=2 E=5 S=9
5+8+6+5+5+2+2+5+1+2+5+9=55
THEY WILL NEED 35 PODDLES.
P=6 O=5 D=4 D=4
L=2 E=5 S=9
6+5+4+4+2+5+9=35
THEY WILL NEED 33
MONCHAS.
M=3 O=5 N=4
C=3 H=8 A=1 S=9
3+5+4+3+8+1+9=33

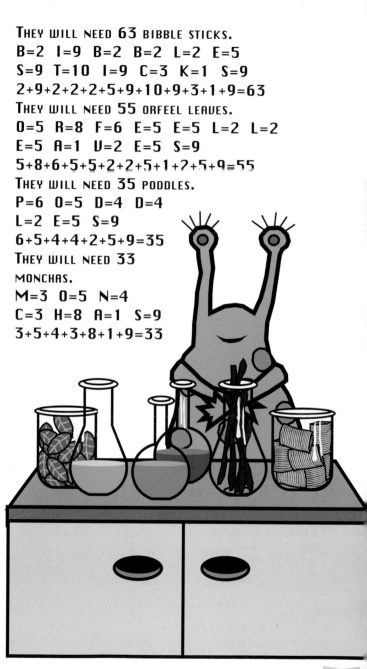

31

24–25 Back on the trail

X

1
2
3
4

A   B   C   D

THEY WILL GO THROUGH SQUARES **1D, 2D, 3D, 4D, 4C, 3C, 3B, 3A, 2A,** AND **1A.**

8+7=15: B
25-15=10: R
4+9=13: A
3×3=9
  (3+3+3=9): M
11+11=22: B
6×10=60
(10+10+10+10+10+10=60): L
12-4=8: E

4×4=16 (4+4+4+4=16): E
13-6=7: G
9×2=18 (2+2+2+2+2+2+2+2+2=18): G
14-3=11: S

7×4=28 (4+4+4+4+4+4+4=28): A
6×6=36 (6+6+6+6+6+6=36): N
4×1=4 (1+1+1+1=4): D

2+6=8: B
3×4=12 (4+4+4=12): A
6+12=18: R
20-4=16: P
2×2=4 (2+2=4): S

26–27 Treasure!

THE SECRET MESSAGE READS: "MIX BRAMBLE EGGS AND BARPS."
2×10=20 (10+10=20): M
5×3=15 (3+3+3+3+3=15): I
11+6=17: X

Good-bye!

"After that adventure, we need a break! Why not join us on our Galaxy Getaway?"